THE GOLDEN BELLS

Two Plays For Advent

BY HENRY SCHOLBERG

C.S.S. Publishing Co., Inc.
Lima, Ohio

THE GOLDEN BELLS

9247 / ISBN 1-55673-452-2   PRINTED IN U.S.A.

——————————————

This book is dedicated to my sisters:

Mrs. Miriam Cook of Sanford, Florida
Mrs. Dorothy Cox of Alva, Florida
Mrs. C. W. Paape of Waterloo, Canada
Dr. Helen Ammons of San Francisco, California

——————————————

Preface

The two plays included in this book are period pieces, the one, *The Bells Of Christmas Eve,* takes place in 1520, and the other, *The Golden Gift*, is set just 300 years later, in 1820. They were not planned that way. It just happened.

Being period pieces, they should be done in appropriate costuming. Minimal technical effects are needed. In *Bells* there should be church bells chiming and rising to a crescendo as the play ends. In *Gift* there are no technical requirements. The narrator indicates the passage of time from the earlier scenes to the last scene. However, during the reading of Jean Valjean's letter, it is effective for soft organ music to be playing "Silent Night, Holy Night."

Since one play takes place in Italy and the other in France, it is recommended that the director, if not conversant in the appropriate language of the play under production, seek advice from someone who is fluent in Italian or French.

Normally, applause follows the performance of a play — even one that is done within the sacred walls of a church. However, the solemnity with which *Bells* ends makes applause seem out of place, and the audience should be asked silently to contemplate the message of the play they have just seen.

Both of these plays have been performed, and each was successfully and enthusiastically received; so anyone wishing to present them can be assured that "they work." *The Golden Gift* was presented in 1977 and again in 1990, and *The Bells Of Christmas Eve* had its world premiere in 1989.

Break a leg.

The Bells Of Christmas Eve

The Cast
(in order of speaking)

Sebastiano Franco
Sister Sophia
Bruder Hans
Antonio
Francesca
Mario Marchesi
Pietro Vermelli
Giuseppe

Synopsis

Scene The First
in which Father Sebastiano Franco is bemoaning the non-ringing of the church bells on Christmas Eve and is visited by a panic-stricken nun and a strange monk from Germany.

Scene The Second
in which a girl and her brother stumble upon a man dying in the cold.

Scene The Third
in which a rich man and a poor man commit insufficient acts of love.

Scene The Fourth
in which a little boy with a noble and loving heart removes a curse.

About The Play

It takes place in 1520 in a small village in Alpine Italy at a time of intolerance when persons accused of witchcraft or heresy were often burned at the stake. This occurred in both the Roman Catholic and Protestant camps; so neither camp can take pride in this chapter of its past.

A Final Note

This is a play which does not lend itself to a curtain call or applause at its conclusion. After the service, the cast members will greet you as you leave the sanctuary, and you may express your feelings to them at that time.

The Bells Of Christmas Eve

Scene The First

in which Father Sebastiano Franco is bemoaning the non-ringing of the church bells on Christmas Eve, and is visited by a strange monk from Germany.

(Franco is seated at his desk writing. He appears agitated, gets up, goes to the window, looks up and mutters:)

FRANCO: They are not ringing. The bells are not ringing. Why? *(He shrugs.)* I suppose Guido is . . . *(He shakes his head resignedly and goes back to his desk. There is a knock on the door. He hopes that by ignoring it, it will somehow go away. A second knock.) Entre! Entre!*

SOPHIA: *(Entering, out of breath) Buona sera, Padre.*

FRANCO: *Buona Sera,* Sister Sophia. Did you come all the way from the convent in order to bid me good evening? As you can see, I am preparing for Christmas Eve mass —

SOPHIA: It's — it's —

FRANCO: It's a problem, I know. Why must you always have problems at the most inconvenient times?

SOPHIA: It's more than a problem, *Padre.* It's — an emergency.

FRANCO: Emergency? What sort of emergency?

SOPHIA: Well — uh —

FRANCO: Come come, Sister Sophia. How can I respond to this emergency of yours if I don't know what it is? .

SOPHIA: The bells are not ringing.

FRANCO: That is not an emergency. There is a reason for it. Guido, the bell ringer, is not ringing the bells because he is drunk —

SOPHIA: But he —

FRANCO: — so to resolve this little problem of yours — or emergency, as you call it — you must go to his house, throw a bucket of ice water in his face and tell him to go ring the bells.

SOPHIA: But he is there. He is at the church.

FRANCO: What?!

SOPHIA: He pulls the rope down. Then it goes up. He pulls it down. Then it goes up. He pulls it —

FRANCO: Please!

SOPHIA: But no sound comes out.

FRANCO: What?!

SOPHIA: No sound comes out.

FRANCO: I heard you. There must be a reason. Perhaps the rope is not properly attached. Did it occur to anyone present to climb up the bell tower to check on the rope?

SOPHIA: I did that myself. The rope went down and it went up. It went —

FRANCO: Yes, yes. This is serious. I shall have to go there and see for myself.

HANS: *(Entering)* That will not be necessary.

FRANCO: How did you get in?

HANS: Through the door. It was unlocked.

FRANCO: Who are you, and what are you doing here?

HANS: I am a servant of the living Christ.

FRANCO: What is your order? Dominican? Franciscan? Augustinian?

HANS: I belong to no particular order.

FRANCO: Then you must be of some heretical sect.

HANS: I belong to no particular order.

FRANCO: Your name? Surely your dear mother must have given you a name.

HANS: I am *Bruder* Hans.

FRANCO: A-hah! A German! Then you must be a follower of that greatest heretic of them all: Dr. Luther.

HANS: My loyalty is to God, and to none other.

FRANCO: Then what brings you to this house and this parish on this very cold night?

HANS: I came to tell you it is not necessary for you to climb up the bell tower.

FRANCO: And why, may I ask, not?

HANS: Because I know why the Christmas bells do not ring; so it is not necessary for you to climb to the top of the bell tower.

FRANCO: Why not?

HANS: There is a curse on this village and this parish.

FRANCO: I cannot accept that.

SOPHIA: Holy Mary, Mother of God!

HANS: Sister Sophia.

SOPHIA: Yes, *Bruder* Hans?

HANS: I understand it was you who climbed the stairs to the top of the bell tower.

SOPHIA: Yes.

HANS: Tell me, Sister Sophia, when Guido was pulling the rope —

SOPHIA: Down and up. Down and —

HANS: Yes. When Guido was pulling the rope, did the bells swing as they will do when the rope is pulled down and up, down and up?

SOPHIA: Yes. Yes, they did.

HANS: Did you take time to notice if the clappers —

SOPHIA: Clappers?

HANS: Yes. Those things inside the bells that make them go ding dong.

SOPHIA: Is that what they're called?

HANS: Yes.

SOPHIA: I didn't know that.

HANS: Did you notice if the clappers might have been missing?

SOPHIA: They were not missing, but — no ding dong.

HANS: Well, Father Sebastiano Franco?

FRANCO: What can I say?

HANS: You can ask why.

FRANCO: Very well. Why? Why is there a curse on this town?

HANS: Do you remember the widow Fruzzetti?

FRANCO: Of course. She was convicted of witchcraft.

SOPHIA: And burned at the stake.

HANS: She was innocent.

FRANCO: She was convicted in the court of the Grand Inquisitor.

SOPHIA: Her only crime was her beauty.

FRANCO: The Grand Inquisitor himself pronounced sentence.

HANS: The Grand Inquisitor was a fiend.

FRANCO: He was an agent of His Holiness Pope Leo X.

HANS: He was an agent of the anti-Christ.

FRANCO: Bite your tongue!

HANS: It would not surprise me to learn that he is the anti-Christ himself. If one were to shave his head, one might find the number six-six-six tattooed on his scalp.

SOPHIA: The sign of the beast. Holy Mary, Mother of God!

FRANCO: I can listen to no more of this.

HANS: Maria Fruzzetti was a handsome, full-breasted woman, was she not?

FRANCO: Yes, Oh, yes!

HANS: But there were men — husbands — in your parish who lusted after her.

FRANCO: Go on.

HANS: But she resisted their lust; so they conspired to accuse her of having bewitched them. And, of course, the wives of these men — in their jealousy — were only too happy to perjure themselves by testifying against the poor woman.

FRANCO: You have said enough. I must ask you to leave.

HANS: Do you remember the burning? As the flames rose and the smoke entered her lungs, she let out a great cry.

SOPHIA: I remember.

HANS: That was the curse.

FRANCO: Say no more.

HANS: Would you like the curse to be lifted?

FRANCO: Let us say you are right. I am not saying you are, mind you. But for the moment let us say you are right. What must be done to lift the curse?

HANS: The murder — and that's what it was: murder — of *Signora* Fruzzetti was a great act of hatred. It must be countermanded by an equally great act of love. A miracle of love, if you will.

FRANCO: Can you be more specific?

HANS: I will take my leave now. It is for you and your parishioners to find in your hearts the love that will remove the curse. *(He exits.)*

FRANCO: Well, Sister Sophia. You knew the widow Fruzzetti well. Do you believe she was a witch?

SOPHIA: She was no more a witch than I am.

FRANCO: Oh?

SOPHIA: She was a loyal daughter of the church. She was my friend, and I loved her as a friend. And when she screamed as the flames rose, I prayed that I might take her place.

FRANCO: You can not do that. We must think of an act of love to countermand that terrible act that sentenced her to death.

SOPHIA: *(After a pause)* I have an idea.

FRANCO: My dear Sister Sophia. If you have a hundred ideas, I will hear them all.

SOPHIA: There is Mario Marchesi.

FRANCO: The merchant?

SOPHIA: If he were to give two or three gold florins to the poor box, perhaps —

FRANCO: *Magnifico!* Summon him at once! But say nothing to him of the poor box. Leave that to me. *(She exits.)* Five gold florins. We'll make it five gold florins, *Signor* Marchesi.

Scene The Second

in which a girl and her little brother stumble upon an old man dying in the cold.

(Tonio and his big sister Cesca are trudging along to the village church. An old man, Giuseppe the baker, is lying in their path.)

TONIO: It is so cold!

CESCA: Hurry. The church will be warm. Others will be there.

TONIO: Why aren't the bells ringing?

CESCA: I don't know.

TONIO: But they always ring on Christmas Eve.

CESCA: I said I don't know why they aren't ringing.

16

TONIO: Who is this?

CESCA: It is Giuseppe the baker. He has fallen by the wayside.

TONIO: We must help him, Cesca.

CESCA: What can we do? He is too heavy to lift. There is no one close by to help us.

TONIO: I will stay by him. My body will keep him warm.

CESCA: But you will freeze to death yourself.

TONIO: No. I'll be all right. Cover us up with my cloak. But hurry. Hurry to the village and bring help for the old man.

CESCA: I will hurry, Tonio. I will hurry. *(She exits.)*

Scene The Third

in which a rich man and a poor man commit acts of love which are insufficient.

(Father Franco is in his study writing.)

MARIO: *(Entering) Buona sera, Padre! Buon Natale!*

FRANCO: Ah, yes! *Entre, Signor* Marchesi. *Buon Natale!*

MARIO: You sent for me, *Padre?*

FRANCO: Yes. Would you care for some wine?

MARIO: Not now. I must return to my family. We are opening gifts this evening, and I want to see the smiles on my children's faces when they see the gifts I bought them. Mighty expensive ones, I tell you.

FRANCO: That must be a great joy.

MARIO: I believe you did send for me.

FRANCO: Yes. This is a very delicate matter.

MARIO: How much?

FRANCO: I beg your pardon.

MARIO: How many florins do you need for this new project of yours. What is it this time? A new orphanage? A home for wayward girls? A —?

FRANCO: It is nothing like that, but it is hard to explain.

MARIO: It is getting late, and my family is waiting for me.

FRANCO: The bells of Christmas Eve are not ringing.

MARIO: I have noticed that, and I wish to know why. I have given good money to the upkeep of the church, and I expect to see a decent return of my investments.

FRANCO: Our village and our parish are cursed.

MARIO: Cursed? What kind of a curse?

FRANCO: Do you remember the Fruzzetti woman?

MARIO: Ah, yes. A most beautiful wom — Uh — she was burned at the stake, was she not?

FRANCO: I have received confirmation that she was innocent of the crime of witchcraft.

18

MARIO: But she was condemned by the Grand Inquisitor himself.

FRANCO: It seems he made a grievous error.

MARIO: Who informed you of all this?

FRANCO: Uh — An emissary of his Holiness the Pope.

MARIO: How does this concern me? I am completely innocent in the matter of Maria's — of the widow Fruzzetti's trial and execution.

FRANCO: As she was dying, she cried out loudly —

MARIO: I remember.

FRANCO: — a curse that the bells of our church would never again ring announcing the birth of our Lord. And the only way that the curse can be lifted is for someone in our parish to commit a great act of love.

MARIO: And I am to perform that act?

FRANCO: Exactly.

MARIO: What must I do?

FRANCO: A generous contribution to the poor box would be —

MARIO: Done! I could donate a few ducats?

FRANCO: A few ducats?! My dear friend, it must be an act of great love. I was thinking more in terms of 500 florins.

MARIO: Five hundred florins! I am a poor man! It is true I own some property. But 500 florins!

FRANCO: An act of great love. I'm afraid a few ducats would simply not do.

MARIO: Can you guarantee that five gold florins will make the bells ring?

FRANCO: I am quite certain of that.

MARIO: Will you let it be known throughout the parish that it was I who lifted the curse and made the bells ring?

FRANCO: Be assured of that.

MARIO: Five hundred, eh?

FRANCO: Five hundred.

MARIO: Very well. I have in my purse five gold florins — each worth 100 florins. Bring the poor box.

FRANCO: Here it is, but first let me consecrate the gift. *In nomine patris et filii et spiritus sancti. Amen.* I present your precious and generous child, Mario Marchesi, who is about to perform a most magnificent act of love. I then consecrate this gift to the poor and ask your divine blessing on him and on it and that through it the terrible curse on our parish will be lifted. Amen.

MARIO: Amen. *(He puts the gold florins in the box one by one.)*

FRANCO: *Uno. Due. Tre. Quattro. (Pause and hesitation.) Cinque. (They both rush to the window and look up. No bells.)*

MARIO: You guaranteed it!

FRANCO: I only said I was quite certain —

MARIO: You are a fraud! I demand my money back!

FRANCO: That is quite impossible. Once money enters the poor box, it can be released only by a certificate from the archbishop. I shall write to him at once if you wish.

MARIO: How long will it take?

FRANCO: Several months, I'm afraid. He lives in Milan.

MARIO: Bah! You are a fiend — a charlatan! *(He goes to the exit and bumps into Pietro who is entering.)* Out of my way, fool! *(He exits.)*

PIETRO: *Buona sera, Padre. Buon Natale!*

FRANCO: *Buon Natale,* Pietro, my brother! What brings you to my door on such a cold night?

PIETRO: The bells are not ringing.

FRANCO: I am keenly aware of that, Pietro.

PIETRO: Why? I am told that our village is famous throughout Italy for the beautiful bells that on Christmas Eve announce the birth of our Blessed Lord.

FRANCO: The bells do not ring because of a curse —

PIETRO: A curse?

FRANCO: It is a long story and not a very happy one to relate. *(Pause)* But I have just thought of a way in which we might lift that curse, and it includes you, my son.

PIETRO: Me?

FRANCO: You. You have not traveled much in your lifetime, have you?

PIETRO: I have barely gone beyond this village.

FRANCO: How would you like to travel to Rome?

PIETRO: I have a cousin in Naples and an uncle in Florence and a second cousin in — Rome?!

FRANCO: I am sending you to Rome on a pilgrimage.

PIETRO: But I have no money for such a long journey. I am but a poor cobbler.

FRANCO: Money is no object. We have just received a gift of — of 300 florins for the poor box —

PIETRO: But if it's for the poor —

FRANCO: I'm sure the poor will not mind if they know it is to be used for such a noble purpose.

PIETRO: It is my understanding that money cannot be taken out of the poor box without a certificate from the archbishop.

FRANCO: That is a common misconception.

PIETRO: How will my pilgrimage to Rome make the bells ring?

FRANCO: You will carry a message to His Holiness Pope Leo and request him to intercede for us and say a special mass for the removal of the curse.

PIETRO: I will actually have an audience with His Holiness?!

FRANCO: To put it another way, he will have an audience with you.

PIETRO: But the journey will take several months. We want the bells to ring tonight.

FRANCO: I've thought of that. Now, before I give you the 200 florins —

PIETRO: I believe you said 300.

FRANCO: Did I? I believe I misspoke.

PIETRO: Oh.

FRANCO: So before I give you the 200 florins and before you pack your belongings for the pilgrimage, I will consecrate you to your task.

PIETRO: Will that make the bells ring?

FRANCO: I'm quite sure. Kneel. *In nomine patris et filii et spiritus sancti, Amen.* This is your devoted and humble servant Pietro Vermelli who is about to make a most hazardous pilgrimage to Rome. I consecrate him to your love and care, and pray our Holy Mother will guide and protect him on his journey. Amen. *(They both rush to the window and look up. No bells.)*

PIETRO: No bells.

FRANCO: I'm sorry, my son. *(Cesca enters breathlessly.)*

CESCA: Please, *Padre.* You must come quickly.

FRANCO: Francesca! What is it?

CESCA: On the north road. There is a man lying on the road.

FRANCO: What man? Who is he?

CESCA: He is Giuseppe the baker. He must have fallen. My brother is lying beside him to keep him warm. Hurry! Or they will both freeze to death!

FRANCO: Quick, Pietro. Go to your house and bring two blankets.

PIETRO: But I have only one blanket.

FRANCO: Then go to the home of *Signor* Marchesi and get them from him.

PIETRO: What if he will not give?

FRANCO: Then tell him his soul will be consumed to the flames of eternal hell. Go. *(Pietro goes.)*

CESCA: We must hurry! *(They exit.)*

Scene The Fourth

in which a little boy with a noble and loving heart removes a curse.

GIUSEPPE: I am cold. Very cold. Who is this? It is little Antonio. What is he doing here? He's just a little boy. Two days ago he was begging for sweet cakes, and I yelled at him and chased him away. Sleep well, little boy. *(Enter Cesca, Franco and Pietro.)*

CESCA: There they are.

FRANCO: Giuseppe, are you all right?

GIUSEPPE: Yes. I am all right, but what is little Antonio doing here?

FRANCO: He lay down beside you to keep you warm. You should be grateful. He may have saved your miserable life.

CESCA: Something is wrong, *Padre*. Tonio is cold and stiff. His eyes are open, but he doesn't answer me. Please see to him, *Padre*.

FRANCO: Wake up, Antonio. *(Pause, as he examines him.)* You must be brave, Francesca. Your little brother is dead.

CESCA: No! He can't be!

FRANCO: Be strong, my child.

CESCA: Oh, God! How could you be so cruel to take my little brother?

HANS: *(Entering)* Our God, who gave your brother a loving and noble heart, is not cruel.

FRANCO: I will say a prayer for his soul. *In nomine —*

HANS: There is no need of that. At this very moment he is in the arms of Jesus. Listen. *(The bells are ringing softly. Franco continues to pray silently.)*

PIETRO: God be praised!

GIUSEPPE: I am in the twilight of my years. He was at the very dawn of his. Yet he gave his life for me.

HANS: Greater love hath no man than this: that a man would give up his life for a friend. Our Master said that. But this boy gave up his life for a man he hardly knew. How Jesus must love him!

SOPHIA: *(Entering) Padre!* The bells are ringing!

FRANCO: We hear them!

SOPHIA: But Guido is not ringing them. He is in the tavern.

FRANCO: If he is not ringing them, who is?

SOPHIA: No one. They are ringing by themselves. It is a miracle! *(Bells are now playing loudly and joyously. One by one, the actors leave the stage. Cesca and Tonio are the last to exit.)*

The Golden Gift

A **Christmas play based on a scene from** *Les Misérables* **by Victor Hugo**

Program Notes

Our play is based on an incident which comes early in one of Victor Hugo's greatest novels, *Les Misérables* — ("The Wretched Ones").

This book was published while Hugo was in exile in England in 1862. It was written as a social novel in which he made society itself the heavy in the piece. The novel was received with mixed reactions. One reviewer called it "his pernicious book." Another more charitably wrote: "It is . . . the master work of fiction of this century. There are things in it quite wonderful."

In his own defense, Hugo said: "Society is to blame for tolerating prisons where innocent but unfortunate men enter to quit them hardened ruffians. Society is to blame for not acknowledging that wretched women take to the streets to prove their virtue. We can make no other teaching."

One of his most famous sayings was: *"Les galères font le galérien."* Translation: "Prisons make the criminal."

The story of the good Bishop Bienvenue and the ex-convict Jean Valjean which we are about to enact for you occurs in the French Alpine region on a cold night in 1815. Using poetic license, we have rewritten it as taking place in the Yule season and done it as a Christmas play. It seemed to us that the moral thrust of the story lent itself to the Christmas theme.

As we watch the play, let us listen as Jean Valjean tells his tragic story and ask ourselves: What is Victor Hugo saying to us today?

— The Author

27

The Cast
(in order of speaking)

Narrator
Mademoiselle Arlette
Monseigneur Bienvenue
Jean Valjean
Maria
Anna
Roger
René
Philippe
The Gendarme

The Golden Gift

Scene One

NARRATOR: The play you are about to see is based on a chapter in *Les Misérables,* a novel by the French writer Victor Hugo. The title of his novel is difficult to translate into English. It means "the miserable ones," "the wretches," "the outcasts."

Some changes have been made. For example, the candlesticks in Hugo's story are made of silver, but the rest of the story and the message are essentially unchanged. In fact, some of the dialogue is taken directly from the book itself.

The first scene opens with Bishop Bienvenue sitting in his rocking chair, reading his Bible. He is reading his favorite passage, the Sermon on the Mount, the part where Jesus tells us to forgive our enemies, to love those who hate us, and to go the second mile. *(His name, Bienvenue, incidentally, means "welcome.")*

Suddenly his niece, Mlle. Arlette Baptistine, bursts into the room and says:

ARLETTE: Do you know what day it is today?

BISHOP: Um — Thursday, I think.

ARLETTE: No, Uncle! What *day.*

BISHOP: The eighth. December eighth.

ARLETTE: And what is special about December 8th, 1815?

BISHOP: Ah! Let me think. It's not your birthday. That comes in October. It's not mine. I've ceased having birthdays.

29

ARLETTE: I'll give you a hint. It's an anniversary of something.

BISHOP: Now I should get it. Um — December 8th. The Battle of Waterloo. No. That was only six months ago.

ARLETTE: No, no, Uncle. It's more personal than that.

BISHOP: Ah! My dear niece. This tired old brain of mine will have to give up.

ARLETTE: Very well. Today is the 10th anniversary of your becoming a bishop.

BISHOP: So it is! December 8th, 1805. Has it been 10 years?!

ARLETTE: Yes! I shall get some wine. We must observe the occasion properly.

BISHOP: Did I ever tell you how I happened to be appointed bishop? My meeting with Napoleon?

ARLETTE: Many times. But I never tire of the hearing just as you never tire of the telling.

BISHOP: I was curé of Brignolles at the time. I had gone to Paris on some business to do with my curacy, and I was waiting in the ante-chamber of Cardinal Fesch. Suddenly the door burst open, and in walked the Emperor Napoleon himself. He, too, had business with the cardinal. I stood up and found myself staring at him in spite of myself. He was short of stature. He had dark, piercing eyes. He stood before me and said, "Who is this good man who looks at me?" Without thinking I said, "Sire, you behold a good man, and I a great one. Each of us may profit by it." A slight smile came to his face. He shook my hand and, without saying a word, went in to see the cardinal. It was not long after this that I learned that I had been appointed bishop of Devereaux. Apparently, he had asked the cardinal who I was, and, well —

ARLETTE: Oh, Uncle. You have told that story many times, but that is the first time he shook your hand.

BISHOP: As I recall, he extended his hand and —

ARLETTE: You are hopeless, and I love you. I predict that in five years he will embrace you and kiss you on both cheeks.

BISHOP: What are you saying, my dear?

ARLETTE: To Napoleon, then. Your benefactor.

BISHOP: *Vive l'Empereur!*

ARLETTE: This is not good wine.

BISHOP: It is adequate.

ARLETTE: You could do better, you know.

BISHOP: But — it is adequate.

ARLETTE: Adequate! The chair you are sitting in is adequate. This table is adequate. All the furniture in this house is adequate. This house itself is adequate.

BISHOP: Arlette!

ARLETTE: Why can't we live in the Bishop's Palace that was intended for you? Oh, no! You had to exchange it for a tiny hospital with six small rooms.

BISHOP: Please don't go on like this, Arlette. A moment ago you were so pleasant — so convivial.

ARLETTE: I'm not finished. Your salary. Fifteen thousand francs. And what have you done with it?

BISHOP: I know what I've done with it.

ARLETTE: Fourteen thousand to this charity or that charity: prison reform, seminaries, maternity hospitals and whatnot. And how much for the most important charity of them all — yourself? One thousand francs!

BISHOP: It is sufficient.

ARLETTE: Sufficient?! If it were not for my small inheritance, we would starve. If you can't think of yourself, think of me.

BISHOP: Come here. I want to show you something. What do you see here?

ARLETTE: It is the manger scene.

BISHOP: What do you *see?*

ARLETTE: The Holy Family. The Virgin, Joseph and the Infant.

BISHOP: The Infant.

ARLETTE: Jesus.

BISHOP: What does it all mean?

ARLETTE: It is the Nativity of Our Lord.

BISHOP: More than that. It is God's gift. God's gift to us. To you and to me. He loved us so much that he gave part of himself to us. Now do you understand?

ARLETTE: What does all this have to do with what we are talking about?

BISHOP: How can we grumble about what we have when God was so generous with us?

ARLETTE: I still don't understand.

BISHOP: A few weeks ago I preached a sermon on this very subject. I talked about property and how we are only stewards of whatever property we may think we possess. All things come from God, I said, and our custody lasts only for the short period of our lifetime. Do you remember that sermon?

ARLETTE: I — I think so.

BISHOP: Um — And I thought it was one of my better sermons.

ARLETTE: It's all very well for you to talk about stewardship, but there are some things I like to think we possess.

BISHOP: Everything we have comes from God. Even if we make something for ourselves, God gave us the materials to make it with, and the talent to make it.

ARLETTE: These candlesticks.

BISHOP: They are beautiful, aren't they?

ARLETTE: I remember Grandmama — your own mother — saying how proud she was of them.

BISHOP: I have to admit my human frailties. I hope I never have to part with them.

ARLETTE: Then you are human, after all.

BISHOP: Very human. And my very human stomach informs me that it is supper time.

ARLETTE: I'll see if it is ready. Oh! I was talking with Madame Cartier today.

BISHOP: Madame Cartier! And what news did Madame Cartier impart to you that you are about to impart to me?

ARLETTE: There is a stranger in Domène.

BISHOP: Oh?

ARLETTE: He is a convict.

BISHOP: A convict? How do you know?

ARLETTE: He carries a yellow passport. He tried to get food and lodging at La Barre's *auberge*, but was turned away. Then he went to the jail and asked the turnkey to let him stay there, but was refused again.

BISHOP: Poor fellow!

ARLETTE: Poor fellow, indeed! Probably a thief or cutthroat.

BISHOP: Where is he now?

ARLETTE: I hope he is on his way to Grenoble.

BISHOP: Grenoble is not far, but it is dark and cold out, and the mountain roads are treacherous.

ARLETTE: All the doors in Domène are being locked tonight. We should do the same.

BISHOP: We agreed it was supper time.

ARLETTE: I think it's ready. *(She exits. Bishop returns to his Bible. There is a knock on the door. Bishop opens it.)*

BISHOP: *Entrez. (Jean Valjean enters.)*

JEAN: My name is Jean Valjean. I am a convict; I have been 19 years in the galleys. Four days ago I was set free. During those four days I have walked from Toulon. Today I have walked 12 leagues. When I reached this place this evening, I went to an *auberge,* and they sent me away on account of my yellow passport. I went to another *auberge;* they said, "Get out!" I went to the jail, and the turnkey would not let me stay there. I crept into a dog kennel, but the dog bit me and drove me away. Finally, I went to the square where I lay down on a stone bench. A good woman showed me your house and said, "Knock there." What is this place? Are you an *auberge?* I have money. I am tired and hungry. Can I stay? *(During these lines Arlette has entered.)*

BISHOP: Arlette, put on another plate. We have company.

ARLETTE: But, Uncle, this is the man who —

BISHOP: Just do it. *(She stomps off in a huff, but returns to set the table angrily.)* You will join us, *Monsieur?*

JEAN: This isn't a joke, is it? This is my passport — yellow, as you see. That is enough to have me kicked out wherever I go. I will read it to you. I learned how to read in the galleys. There is a school there for those who care for it. See, here is what they put in my passport: "Jean Valjean, a liberated convict, native of Faverolles, has been 19 years in the galleys; five years for burglary; 14 for having attempted four times to escape. This man is dangerous." There you have it. Everybody has thrust me out. Will you receive me?

BISHOP: Arlette, when we have finished eating, you will put some sheets on the bed in the alcove.

ARLETTE: Uncle!

JEAN: True? You will keep me? You won't drive me away? A convict! You call me *Monsieur* and don't say, "Get out, dog!" as everyone else does. I thought you would send me away; so I told you first off who I am. Tonight I shall have a bed — with a mattress and sheets — like other people. It is 19 years since I slept in a bed. Are you really willing that I should stay? You are good people. I can pay, you know? You are an innkeeper, aren't you?

BISHOP: I am a priest.

JEAN: A priest? Ah, then you will not ask money.

BISHOP: No. Keep your money. How much have you?

JEAN: One hundred and nine francs.

BISHOP: One hundred and nine francs! How long did it take you to earn that?

JEAN: Nineteen years!

BISHOP: Shall we have supper? It seems to be ready. *(Jean goes for the middle seat.)*

ARLETTE: You will sit there. *(She wants him to be as far away as possible.)*

BISHOP: She wants you to be as close to the fireplace as possible. *(They all sit. As Bishop says grace, Jean dives in with both hands. Arlette watches shyly. He discovers his faux pas and tries to recover.)* In the name of the Father, the Son and the Holy Spirit. We thank thee for this food. Bless it to our use and thus to thy service. Amen.

JEAN: You are very good to me. You don't despise me. You take me into your house.

BISHOP: Ah! There is something missing. *(He gets the candlesticks, puts them on the table.)* I shall light them in honor of our guest. There.

JEAN: Gold.

BISHOP: Yes, indeed!

JEAN: *(With mouth full)* Knzz rmmsmm.

BISHOP: I beg your pardon.

JEAN: They must be worth a king's ransom.

BISHOP: Oh, hardly that. A few thousand francs perhaps.

JEAN: You even light candles for me.

ARLETTE: He is a thief.

BISHOP: Arlette!

ARLETTE: It's true. By his own admission.

BISHOP: But he is our guest.

JEAN: She is right, you know.

ARLETTE: Of course, I am right.

JEAN: I did it for my sister.

ARLETTE: Ha!

JEAN: And her four children.

BISHOP: Do you wish to tell us about it?

JEAN: If you will believe me.

ARLETTE: My uncle will listen, and he will believe. I will not listen, and I will not believe.

BISHOP: He deserves a hearing from us.

ARLETTE: He deserves nothing from us. If anything, we deserve something from him. He devoured more in one minute than both of us put together.

BISHOP: He is our guest, and that is his right. Whatever we have in this house is his just as much as it is ours.

ARLETTE: You are incurable, Uncle. Incurable! I will go to bed now.

BISHOP: Give me a proper kiss, and say good night to our guest.

ARLETTE: *Bonne nuit,* Uncle. *(She kisses him.) Bonne nuit, Monsieur.* I will leave you *gentlemen* to your conversation. *(She exits and slams a door.)*

JEAN: I don't think she likes me.

BISHOP: Oh. It's not that she doesn't like you. She doesn't know you.

JEAN: She doesn't want to know me.

BISHOP: But I do. More wine?

JEAN: Good wine!

BISHOP: I like it.

38

JEAN: I was born in Faverolles. I suppose I told you that.

BISHOP: Yes.

JEAN: My parents died when I was very young. My father had been a pruner; so it was natural that I should be one, too. I lived with my widowed sister and her four children. Since I was in seasonal work, I had to find odd jobs anywhere I could when I wasn't pruning. I worked as a reaper, teamster, common laborer — anything to earn a few francs. Then it happened. It was in the late fall of 1796 — just 19 years ago.

Scene Two

(Through the magic of television, we are now in Faverolles in 1796 in the home of Jean Valjean's sister Maria and her four children, Anne, René, Philippe and Roger.)

JEAN: I had been looking for work all day. Whenever I looked I was told, "We have nothing for you today. Come back tomorrow." I was afraid to come home and face my sister with the bad news. I finally got up enough courage, and when I finally got there it was the same old greeting.

MARIA: Well?

JEAN: Nothing.

MARIA: What do you mean? Nothing.

JEAN: What I said. Nothing. There was no work.

MARIA: Did you try Dominique's livery? You told me they were looking for drivers.

JEAN: They were. But not any more. They hired Jacques and Gaston.

ANNE: Mama, I'm hungry.

MARIA: I'm sorry, dear, there's no food in the pantry, and there's no work for your uncle.

ANNE: But other children have food to eat, why not us?

MARIA: Oh, please! I explained to you a million times. There is no money. There is no work. When there is no work, there is no money; and when there is no money, there is no food on the table.

ANNE: But I'm hungry.

ROGER: Me, too.

RENÉ: I'm hungry, too.

PHILIPPE: When do we eat?

MARIA: *Ta gueule! (That means, "Shut up!" Another way to say it is, Fermez la bouche!'', which means, "Shut your mouth!")*

JEAN: Maria! Don't be harsh with them.

MARIA: Don't be harsh, he says. You're a fine one to say that! You don't have to listen to them whining all day.

RENÉ: I earned some centimes today.

JEAN: Oh? How many centimes?

RENÉ: Ten.

JEAN: Where?

RENÉ: At Isabeau's bakery. He let me sweep out the store.

JEAN: Ten centimes won't feed a family. It won't feed one person. Let's put that in a safe place, and when you've made 10 francs, we'll buy food for everyone with it.

PHILIPPE: I could get work, too.

ROGER: Me, too.

JEAN: You children are too little. If there's no work for men, there's no work for boys. Now, run outside and play. Your mother and I need to talk. *(The children exit.)* I'm going to have to steal.

MARIA: No!

JEAN: Yes! It's the only way. I can't stand to see you and the children starving every day. What's to become of us?

MARIA: What's to become of us if you get caught?

JEAN: I won't get caught.

Scene Three

(We're back in the bishop's house again.)

JEAN: That night, I crept out of the house and made my way to Isabeau's bakery shop. There was a loaf of bread in the window. I smashed the glass with my bare fist, grabbed the bread and ran. I heard shouting: "Stop thief! Stop thief!" and steps behind me.

Well, the *gendarme* caught me. I was hauled before the magistrate and sentenced to five years in the galleys. At the end of four years, it was my turn to escape. We all took turns. We'd all help whoever's turn it was. I was free for two days — if it is freedom to be hunted, to turn your head each moment, to tremble at the least noise, to be afraid of everything, of the smoke of a chimney, the passing of a man, the barking of a dog, the gallop of a horse, the striking of a clock, of the day because you see, and of the night because you do not see. During the evening of the second day I was captured and sentenced to three more years. That made it eight. In my sixth year I attempted it again and hid beneath the keel of a ship in dry dock. This time I resisted, and was given five years instead of three. That made it 13 all together. In my 10th year I tried again, but with even less success. Another three years. That made it 16.

Finally, in my 13th year I tried a fourth time but was caught after four hours. Another three years. That made it 19. Four days ago I was given 109 francs and set free. I have had nothing to eat in that time — until now — and have walked all the way from Toulon. Here I am.

BISHOP: Nineteen years for one loaf of bread! Tell me, are you on your way to see your sister?

JEAN: While I was living in the galleys, news reached me that she was living in Grenoble with her youngest child Roger. She was employed as a folder and stitcher at a book bindery. That was 10 years ago. I hope she is still there.

BISHOP: You have suffered a terrible injustice. You are welcome to stay here as long as you like.

JEAN: I cannot do that. I must find my sister, if she still lives. I will be on my way in the morning.

BISHOP: What will you do after you find your sister, or after you satisfy yourself that you can't?

JEAN: I don't know. I will find something. I am grateful to you for what you have done for me, but I need more than one meal in my belly and one night in a bed. I need money. I have to buy good clothes so that people will accept me at inns and not ask for my passport.

BISHOP: What we have here is yours. We want to help you all we can.

JEAN: You are kind, Father, but —

BISHOP: I have a rule that I retire early. I believe it was the American, Dr. Franklin, who said, "Early to bed and early to rise makes a man healthy, wealthy and wise." Only I am told that in English it rhymes. So if you will excuse me. You may wish to warm yourself by the fire a while longer before going to bed. Your room is at the head of the stairs. *Bonne nuit, Monsieur.*

JEAN: *Bonne nuit,* Father. *(Bishop exits. Jean contemplates the candlesticks a while, and, after a certain amount of soul-searching, decides to steal them. After he leaves, the door slams, and that brings Arlette on stage.)*

ARLETTE: The candlesticks! Oh, *mon dieu!* The candlesticks! Uncle! Uncle! Come quickly. *(Bishop enters.)*

BISHOP: What is it, my dear?

ARLETTE: He has gone. Our *guest* has left. He has stolen the candlesticks.

BISHOP: No! No! That cannot be. He could have taken anything else in the house, but not my candlesticks.

ARLETTE: And now, perhaps, you understand the folly of your views on stewardship.

BISHOP: One must ask oneself: where does gold come from?

ARLETTE: Gold! Who cares about where gold comes from? The candlesticks came from Grandmama.

BISHOP: Yes. They were hers. Then they were mine. Now they are his.

ARLETTE: Here we are, engaging in a philosophical discussion of ownership, and the thief is getting farther away by the minute!

BISHOP: My feelings are —

ARLETTE: Are you going to notify the *gendarmerie,* or shall I?

BISHOP: I hardly think that is necessary. Our friend is off to a good start. By the time we notified the *gendarmerie*, he would be half way to Grenoble.

ARLETTE: Our friend! I shall notify the *gendarmes.*

BISHOP: No, Arlette. In the morning, if you still feel the need to do so, you may. For now, let it suffice that we pray for the man's soul.

ARLETTE: *Bonne nuit,* Uncle. *(She stomps out. There is a loud knocking. The Bishop opens the door and in comes Jean with the gendarme, Paul Beauchamp.)*

BISHOP: *Entrez, Messieurs.*

PAUL: I found this man slinking behind your house. He looked suspicious; so I — *(Arlette enters.)*

ARLETTE: I see you managed to catch him. Did he trip over you as you slept?

PAUL: No! Oh, no, *Mademoiselle!* I found him slinking behind your house; so I asked to see his passport. As he was showing it to me, these fell out of his rucksack.

ARLETTE: Our candlesticks!

PAUL: I recognized them at once. I had seen them when I was here once before.

ARLETTE: We, my Uncle and I, are most grateful to you, *Monsieur.*

PAUL: If there is nothing further, I will take this wretch to the jail.

ARLETTE: *Bonne nuit, Monsieur.*

BISHOP: *Un moment, s'il vous plait.*

PAUL: *Oui, Monseigneur.*

BISHOP: On what charge?

PAUL: I do not understand.

BISHOP: You say you are taking him to jail. Is it not the law that some charge must be brought against those we put behind bars?

PAUL: Burglary. He will be charged with burglary.

BISHOP: That is not possible.

PAUL: I still do not comprehend.

BISHOP: He did not steal these candlesticks. They are his. I gave them to him.

PAUL: *Monseigneur.* Your niece, *Mademoiselle* Arlette, said —

BISHOP: *Mademoiselle* is not custodian of these candlesticks.

ARLETTE: He stole them. As surely as there are saints in heaven, he stole them; and I will sign the charges against him if my uncle will not.

BISHOP: I will not tolerate impertinence! Go to your room — at once! *(She bursts into tears, goes stomping out again.)*

PAUL: You *gave* them to him?

BISHOP: Release the prisoner.

PAUL: Why would you *give* them to him? He is a convict. He has a yellow passport.

BISHOP: Our Lord, when he told us to love our neighbors, did not say we should love only those who do not carry yellow passports.

PAUL: I don't know much about these matters, Bishop. Are you sure it is all right to — uh —

BISHOP: I am sure.

PAUL: I will go, then. *Bonne nuit, Monseigneur. (He exits.)*

JEAN: He called you "Bishop."

BISHOP: It is a title of vanity. It seems even God's house needs vanity.

JEAN: I'm ashamed. You trusted me. You fed me. I betrayed you.

BISHOP: There is no need to feel ashamed.

JEAN: I will go. I will not bother you again. Your niece will no longer have reason to fear me.

BISHOP: You may stay until morning.

JEAN: I can't do that. I must find my sister. Thank you for —

BISHOP: You have forgotten something.

JEAN: What?

BISHOP: Your candlesticks.

JEAN: No. They are yours.

BISHOP: I gave them to you. At any rate, that's what I told the *gendarme*.

JEAN: They are beautiful!

BISHOP: Take them as a souvenir of me. Think of them as a kindness, and sometime you must pass that kindness on to someone else.

JEAN: Goodbye.

BISHOP: Before you go. In the name of the Father, the Son and the Holy Spirit. This is your child Jean Valjean. So guide his steps that he will never have to wear chains again. Amen. *(Jean exits.)*

Scene Four

NARRATOR: That was five years ago. It is now 1820. Monseigneur Bienvenue lives alone now. *Mademoiselle* Arlette left him shortly after the — uh — incident with the candlesticks and married a young functionary from Grenoble. The Bishop misses Arlette very much. Let's let him tell you about it.

BISHOP: Four years ago (that would have been in 1816) Arlette moved to Grenoble where she married this government worker. The following year she presented her husband with a son and me with a grand nephew. They will be visiting me soon — as they do every Christmas. Whenever they call, Arlette has me tell how I happened to be appointed Bishop. Did I tell you of my meeting with Napoleon and how he embraced me and kissed me on both cheeks?

NARRATOR: He also missed his friend Jean Valjean and wondered what ever became of him. Then one day he got a letter.

BISHOP: I received a letter today from an old friend. He now calls himself *Monsieur* Madeleine. You know him as Jean Valjean.

JEAN'S VOICE OFF STAGE: "I must tell you of a chance incident that occurred shortly after I left you. I was in the town of Montélimar. A fire broke out in a house near where I was sleeping one night. I rushed in and saved two children who were trapped inside. It seems they were the offspring of the captain of the local *gendarmerie*.

"This, of course, made me an immediate hero, and in the excitement no one thought to ask me for my passport.

"With money from the sale of the candlesticks I was able to start a small factory, manufacturing candy for children — which we call *nougats*.

"I changed my name to *Monsieur* Madeleine and have enjoyed enormous success. Last year I was appointed Mayor of the town.

"But I have never told anyone about our meeting in the Christmas season of 1815. Please know that the kindness you did to me has been repaid 100 times over, and I will continue repaying it as long as I live."

Your servant,
Jean Valjean

"P.S. Please greet your niece for me, and tell her she need never cringe in fear of me again." *(There is a knock on the door.)*

BISHOP: Ah! That must be Arlette now. *(Arlette enters, she and the Bishop take a bow. Then Paul and the Narrator enter and take their bows, followed by Maria and her four children. Finally, Jean Valjean enters and takes a bow.)*

———————————————